SEGUN DOMINIC

forever's whisper

First edition

This book was professionally typeset on Reedsy.
Find out more at reedsy.com

Contents

1 The Uninvited Guest   1

2 Echoes in the Dark   4

3 Shadows of the Past   6

4 Fractured Memories   8

5 A Perilous Bargain   10

6 Secrets in the Shadows   12

7 Uninvited Visitor   14

8 A Desperate Escape   16

9 Into the Storm   19

10 Echoes in the Tunnels   22

11 A Web of Lies   25

12 Echoes of Hope   28

One

The Uninvited Guest

The salty spray kissed Amelia's face as she stood on the weathered dock, the rhythmic crash of waves against the pylons a soothing counterpoint to the disquiet gnawing at her. The quaint harbor town of Driftwood Bay, nestled amidst rolling green hills, had been a sanctuary for the past ten years. Here, amidst the comforting familiarity of cobbled streets and flower-filled window boxes, Amelia had built a new life, one shrouded in comfortable anonymity.

Today, the tranquility was shattered. An unsettling email, cryptic in its brevity, had pierced the veil of her carefully constructed normalcy. Three words – "We Know. Remember." – sent a jolt of adrenaline through her. The sender's address, a jumbled mess of symbols, offered no clues. Yet, the message resonated with a chilling certainty, dragging a long-forgotten dread from the recesses of her mind.

Amelia gripped the railing, the worn wood rough against her palm. Memories, long suppressed, flickered to life – a frantic escape, a blood-curdling scream swallowed by the roar of a storm, a desperate struggle for survival. A life she'd meticulously buried under the assumed identity of Amelia Evans, a name as ordinary as the life she'd cultivated.

The rhythmic clip-clop of hooves on cobblestones drew her attention. A horse-drawn carriage emerged from the winding road, its black paint gleaming under the afternoon sun. The driver, a gaunt man with eyes like chips of flint, stopped beside her.

"Amelia Evans?" His voice was a gravelly rasp.

Amelia's throat constricted. "Yes," she managed, her voice barely a whisper.

The man leaned forward, his gaze unwavering. "You have a visitor. At the Blackwood Manor."

Blackwood Manor. The name sent a shiver down her spine. It was a place whispered about in hushed tones, a looming Gothic structure that sat on the outskirts of town, shrouded in an air of mystery. Amelia had always steered clear of it, the unsettling energy it emanated a constant deterrent.

"Who is it?" she croaked, a sliver of hope battling the rising tide of apprehension.

The driver's lips twitched into a humorless smile. "Someone from your past, Ms. Evans. Someone you wouldn't want to keep waiting."

With that, he flicked the reins, and the carriage lurched forward, leaving Amelia teetering on the edge of a precipice. The carefully constructed facade of her life felt precariously close to crumbling, revealing the secrets she'd so desperately tried to keep hidden.

Driven by a morbid curiosity laced with a sliver of fear, Amelia embarked on a walk she knew she couldn't refuse. The path leading to Blackwood Manor snaked through a dense grove of trees, the sunlight barely penetrating the thick canopy. The air hung heavy with an unsettling silence, broken only by the occasional rustle of unseen creatures.

As Amelia emerged from the trees, the imposing form of Blackwood Manor loomed before her. Jagged gargoyles leered down from the crumbling facade, and cobwebs draped the arched windows like malevolent shrouds. With a deep breath, Amelia steeled herself and approached the heavy oak door. The brass knocker, cold and damp beneath her touch, felt like an icy hand reaching from the past.

Hesitantly, she raised her hand and knocked. The sound echoed through the cavernous interior, sending a tremor of unease through her. A tense silence followed, stretching into what felt like an eternity. Then, a slow creaking sound, like the groan of a tortured soul, announced the grudging opening of the door.

Two

Echoes in the Dark

The sliver of light that had sliced through the gloom vanished as the door swung shut with an ominous thud. Amelia stood in the oppressive darkness, the silence thick and suffocating. A faint musty odor, laced with a hint of something metallic, tickled her nostrils.

Tentatively, she reached out a hand, her fingers brushing against rough stone walls. A sliver of moonlight filtering through a high, grimy window offered a faint illumination. Discerning a shadowy shape ahead, Amelia took a hesitant step forward.

"Hello?" she called out, her voice sounding thin and reedy in the vast emptiness.

No answer. Only an unsettling echo that seemed to mock her from the unseen corners of the room.

Taking a deep breath, Amelia fumbled in her purse for her phone, the faint glow from the screen a beacon in the suffocating darkness. The phone's battery indicator blinked a warning – low battery. She cursed under her breath.

With a determined glint in her eyes, Amelia pressed on. The room seemed endless, each step echoing hollowly in the dead air. The floor beneath her feet transitioned from cold stone to rough wooden planks, the change in texture sending a jolt through her.

A sudden gust of wind extinguished the faint moonlight, plunging the room into complete darkness. Panic clawed at Amelia's throat. Blinded and disoriented, she stumbled backward, her hand knocking over a precariously balanced stack of books with a loud clatter.

The sound sent a flurry of movement from the inky blackness ahead. A shape detached itself from the shadows, advancing towards her with a slow, deliberate gait. Amelia's heart hammered against her ribs.

"Who's there?" she stammered, her voice barely a whisper.

The figure stopped a few feet away, its outline barely discernible in the darkness. A low chuckle, devoid of humor, vibrated through the room.

"Amelia," a voice rasped, the sound like dry leaves rustling in the wind. "So good of you to join me."

The voice sent a jolt of recognition through Amelia. A name she'd buried deep within the recesses of her mind, a name synonymous with terror. But it couldn't be. He was supposed to be dead.

Three

Shadows of the Past

"David?" Amelia's voice trembled as she strained to see through the oppressive darkness. The name tasted foreign on her tongue, a relic from a life she'd desperately tried to outrun.

A dry rasp of laughter echoed in the vast emptiness of the room. "In the flesh, Amelia. Although, not quite as much flesh as I used to have."

A faint click sent a sliver of light lancing through the darkness. A flickering gas lamp sputtered to life, casting long, grotesque shadows that danced on the walls. In its harsh illumination, Amelia finally saw him.

David stood a few paces away, his face a roadmap of wrinkles etched by time and hardship. His eyes, once a bright, piercing blue, were now dull and sunken, their gaze holding a chilling intensity. A jagged scar bisected his left cheek, a gruesome testament to their shared past.

A wave of nausea washed over Amelia. The man before her was a chilling specter of the charming, carefree boy she once knew. This was a man hardened by years of hiding, his motives shrouded in an unsettling mystery.

"How are you alive?" she whispered, the words catching in her throat.

David tilted his head, a humorless smile twisting his lips. "Let's just say, I've cheated death more than once, Amelia. But that's not why you're here, is it?"

He gestured towards a plush armchair positioned in a shaft of moonlight that streamed through a grimy window. "Sit. We have much to discuss."

Amelia hesitated, her instincts screaming at her to turn and run. But the cold curiosity that had driven her to Blackwood Manor in the first place, coupled with a sliver of morbid hope, kept her rooted to the spot.

Slowly, cautiously, she approached the chair and sank down, her back ramrod straight. David remained standing, his gaze fixed on her with an unnerving intensity.

"Ten years, Amelia," he began, his voice laced with a bitter amusement. "Ten years you've lived a lie. Ten years you've hidden from the truth."

The words hung heavy in the air, each one a sharp shard of ice piercing through the carefully constructed walls Amelia had built around herself.

"What truth?" she forced out, her voice barely a hoarse whisper.

David's smile stretched wider, revealing a disconcerting glint of madness in his eyes. "The truth about that fateful night. The night everything changed."

Four

Fractured Memories

The mention of "that night" sent a tremor through Amelia. Vivid flashes of fragmented memories assaulted her – a raging storm, a desperate struggle, a bloodcurdling scream. She squeezed her eyes shut, willing the images to recede.

"Don't," David's voice cut through her turmoil, a razor edge of warning. "Don't shut me out. We both need to face what happened."

Amelia opened her eyes, a flicker of defiance igniting within her. "Why are you here, David? After all these years, what do you want from me?"

David's gaze softened for a fleeting moment, a flicker of the boy she once knew battling the shadows in his eyes. "The truth, Amelia. The truth about what happened to us that night."

He began to pace, a restless energy coursing through him. "They think I'm dead," he spat, his voice laced with venom. "Those who are responsible for everything."

A cold dread coiled in Amelia's stomach. Names, long buried, surfaced in her mind – powerful figures who controlled the town with an iron fist. She knew the whispers, the rumors of their dark deeds. But David accusing them... could it be true?

"Who are you talking about, David?" she ventured cautiously.

He stopped pacing, his gaze locking with hers. "The ones who orchestrated the fire. The ones who took everything from us."

The fire. A horrifying memory flickered to life – flames licking at the night sky, the acrid stench of smoke filling her lungs. But there had been an accident, hadn't there? That's what everyone had said.

David's voice cut through her growing confusion. "It was no accident, Amelia. It was murder. They framed me, made it look like I was the one responsible."

A wave of dizziness washed over Amelia. The world tilted on its axis as the carefully constructed narrative of her past began to crumble. If what David said was true, then her entire life had been built on a lie.

"But why?" she whispered, her voice barely audible.

David let out a harsh laugh, devoid of humor. "Because we stumbled upon something we weren't supposed to. Something that threatened their precious empire."

He leaned closer, his voice dropping to a conspiratorial whisper. "They think I don't know what they're hiding. But I do, Amelia. And I won't rest until the truth is exposed."

Five

A Perilous Bargain

Amelia stared at David, her mind reeling. The revelation that the fire had been a deliberate act, not an accident, shattered the fragile peace she'd built for herself. A tremor of fear ran through her. If powerful figures were willing to kill to protect their secrets, what did that mean for her?

"What do you want me to do, David?" she asked, her voice barely a whisper.

David's gaze softened slightly. "Help me expose them, Amelia. Help me bring them to justice."

A spark of defiance ignited within Amelia. The life she'd built in Driftwood Bay, while ordinary, was hers. She wouldn't let these shadows from the past destroy it.

"And what happens then?" she countered, her voice gaining strength. "What happens when the truth is revealed?"

David hesitated, a flicker of uncertainty crossing his features. "I don't know," he admitted finally. "But we can't live in fear forever, Amelia. We owe it to ourselves, to those we lost, to fight for what's right."

His words resonated with Amelia. The memory of the fire, the searing flames that had consumed everything she held dear, fueled a simmering anger within her. She wouldn't let those responsible continue to wield their power in the shadows.

"Alright, David," she said, her voice firm. "I'll help you. But we need a plan."

A slow, predatory smile spread across David's face. "I knew you wouldn't disappoint me, Amelia. And I think I have an idea."

He launched into a whispered explanation, his voice filled with a calculated intensity. Amelia listened intently, a knot of apprehension tightening in her stomach. David's plan was risky, audacious even. It would require them to tread carefully, to navigate a dangerous web of deceit and manipulation.

But as Amelia weighed the risks, a steely resolve settled in her eyes. The life of quiet anonymity she had craved now seemed hollow. It was time to face the ghosts of her past, to fight for the truth, no matter the cost.

"We can do this, David," she declared, her voice ringing with newfound determination. "But we have to be careful. One wrong move and..."

She trailed off, the unspoken threat hanging heavy in the air. David placed a hand on her shoulder, his grip surprisingly strong.

"We'll be careful, Amelia," he vowed. "But more importantly, we'll be prepared. They won't see us coming."

A flicker of unease danced in Amelia's eyes. The path she had embarked on stretched before her, shrouded in uncertainty. But as she gazed into David's determined eyes, a sliver of hope flickered to life. Perhaps, just perhaps, they could expose the truth and find some semblance of peace amidst the ruins of the past.

Six

Secrets in the Shadows

⁂

The following days were a blur of hushed conversations and meticulous planning. Confined within the gloomy walls of Blackwood Manor, Amelia and David meticulously pieced together a strategy.

David, fueled by a relentless determination, revealed the details of his harrowing escape from the fire and his years spent in hiding. He spoke of piecing together fragments of evidence, of the relentless pursuit of the truth that had consumed him.

Amelia, in turn, shared her experiences in Driftwood Bay, the guilt that had shadowed her for years for abandoning her past. A fragile trust began to blossom between them, a bond forged in shared trauma and a yearning for justice.

Their plan was audacious. David, using his knowledge of the town's underbelly, obtained incriminating documents from a local informant – a shady character with a grudge against the powerful elite. The documents hinted at a web of corruption that ran deep, a network of deceit that implicated some of Driftwood Bay's most respected citizens.

The challenge lay in exposing these documents without revealing their own identities. They decided to leak the information anonymously, a digital Robin Hood striking from the shadows.

Amelia, with her tech-savvy background, took charge of creating an anonymous online persona. Late nights were spent hunched over a dusty laptop in the dimly lit confines of the manor, a world of flickering screens and cryptic codes becoming their new battleground.

David, ever the strategist, focused on creating diversions, sowing seeds of doubt and suspicion amongst the ranks of the corrupt. He orchestrated a series of calculated leaks, planting rumors and manipulating situations from the periphery.

As they delved deeper into their plan, a sense of unease gnawed at Amelia. The weight of their actions pressed down on her, the potential consequences a constant source of worry. The quiet anonymity of her life in Driftwood Bay seemed a distant dream, replaced by the perilous thrill of their clandestine operation.

One evening, as they huddled around the faint glow of the gas lamp, a knock shattered the tense silence. David's face paled, his hand instinctively reaching for the hidden weapon strapped to his ankle.

"Who could it be at this hour?" Amelia whispered, her heart hammering against her ribs.

David shook his head, a grim expression etched on his face. "We'll find out," he replied steely, his voice barely a rasp. With a jerk of his head, he motioned for Amelia to stay hidden in the shadows. Cautiously, he approached the door.

Seven

Uninvited Visitor

Amelia's breath hitched in her throat as the heavy oak door creaked open a sliver. The faint glow from the gas lamp cast an eerie silhouette of the figure standing on the doorstep. Her heart hammered against her ribs, a frantic drumbeat echoing in the tense silence.

David's voice, strained and low, reached her from across the room. "Who is it? What do you want?"

A gruff voice, laced with suspicion, responded. "It's Miller. I came looking for you, David."

A cold dread coiled around Amelia's chest. Miller. The name sent a jolt of recognition through her. He was the town sheriff, a man known for his unwavering loyalty to those in power. His unexpected arrival at Blackwood Manor could only spell trouble.

From her hidden vantage point, Amelia watched as David tensed, his hand hovering near the concealed weapon at his ankle. "What brings you here, Sheriff?" he replied, his voice carefully neutral.

"There have been… rumors," Miller hedged, his voice tight. "Whispers about someone digging into old business. Someone stirring up trouble."

David scoffed. "Sounds like someone's been listening a little too closely, Sheriff."

The tension in the room crackled like static electricity. Amelia knew this was a dangerous game David was playing, a delicate dance on the precipice of exposure.

"You know what I'm talking about, Blackwood," Miller pressed, using David's assumed surname. "There are powerful people in this town who don't take kindly to being disturbed."

A flicker of defiance sparked in David's eyes. "Maybe they should have thought about that before they built their house of cards on a foundation of lies."

Miller's jaw clenched, his grip tightening on the unseen object he held in his hand. The silence stretched, thick with unspoken threats.

Suddenly, a loud crash from the back of the house shattered the tense atmosphere. Amelia flinched, her heart leaping into her throat. David swore under his breath, his gaze darting towards the source of the sound.

"What was that?" Miller boomed, his voice laced with suspicion.

David hesitated, his mind racing. Thinking fast, he threw out a careless explanation. "Probably just an old window blowing open in the storm."

A low rumble of thunder echoed in the distance, seemingly punctuating his lie. Miller narrowed his eyes, unconvinced. "You sure about that, Blackwood?"

"Look, Sheriff," David said, his voice hardening. "I appreciate your concern, but I don't have time for your games. Now, if you'll excuse me…"

Before David could finish, Miller lunged forward, his hand darting beneath his coat. A glint of metal flashed in the dim light – a badge, but also something else, something cold and menacing.

Just as Amelia watched in horror, a bloodcurdling scream pierced the night.

Eight

A Desperate Escape

The scream, raw and primal, shattered the fragile calm of Blackwood Manor. Amelia froze, her blood turning to ice in her veins. Her gaze darted between the open doorway, where Sheriff Miller stood bathed in the faint moonlight, and David, crumpled on the floor in a heap, a crimson stain blossoming on his chest.

Panic surged through Amelia. She knew then that their meticulously crafted plan had unraveled, leaving them exposed and vulnerable. Her mind raced, searching for an escape, a way out of the unfolding nightmare.

A guttural growl erupted from Miller's throat. He lunged towards David, his hand reaching for a gun tucked in his holster. In that split second, a primal instinct took over Amelia.

With a shriek that mirrored David's, she snatched a heavy candlestick from a nearby table and flung it with all her might. The brass candlestick connected with a sickening thud on Miller's temple, sending him sprawling backwards.

He lay motionless for a moment, a dark stain blooming on his forehead. Seizing the opportunity, Amelia bolted towards the back of the house, the source of the earlier crash. Her heart hammered against her ribs, a frantic drumbeat echoing in her ears.

The back door hung ajar, revealing a shadowy hallway shrouded in cobwebs and dust. Without hesitation, Amelia plunged into the darkness, the uneven floorboards groaning under her weight. The crash most likely came from here, a desperate act on someone's part to warn them of the approaching danger.

She navigated the dark hallway blindly, her senses on high alert. The stale air hung heavy with the smell of damp earth and something metallic – a chilling reminder of the violence that had just transpired.

A faint sliver of light flickered ahead, offering a beacon of hope. Quickening her pace, Amelia stumbled into a hidden room, a dusty attic crammed with forgotten relics of the past. Moonlight streamed through a grimy skylight, illuminating the cluttered space.

In the corner, huddled beneath a moth-eaten tapestry, she saw a figure. It was a young woman, her face streaked with dirt and tears, her eyes wide with terror.

"Who are you?" Amelia whispered, her voice ragged with exertion.

The girl flinched, but before she could respond, a booming voice echoed from the hallway. "Amelia! There you are!"

It was David, his voice weak but determined. Relief washed over Amelia, quickly replaced by a surge of fresh panic. They couldn't stay here; Miller would be on his feet any minute.

"There's a secret passage out of here," David rasped, clutching his side where the bullet wound bloomed. "Follow me."

He gestured towards a loose brick in the wall, its edges worn smooth from years of use. With trembling hands, Amelia pushed against the brick, revealing a narrow opening just big enough for a person to squeeze through.

"Go," David urged, his voice strained. "I'll hold him off as long as I can."

Amelia hesitated, torn between reason and a desperate loyalty. Leaving David behind felt like abandoning him to certain peril. But she knew they wouldn't both make it if they stayed.

"I'll come back for you," she choked out, her voice thick with emotion.

David offered a weak smile, his face pale. "Don't worry about me. Just get out of here."

With a final look at David's determined face, Amelia squeezed through the opening, the rough brick scraping against her skin. The young woman followed close behind, her movements nimble and silent.

The passage was narrow and damp, the air thick with the smell of mildew. Amelia crawled on her hands and knees, the darkness pressing in on her from all sides. Claustrophobia threatened to engulf her, but she pushed forward, fueled by the adrenaline coursing through her veins.

After what felt like an eternity, the passage opened into a small, forgotten courtyard. Weeds choked the cobblestone path, and the moonlight cast long, eerie shadows from the towering walls that surrounded them.

The young woman, her eyes wide with fear, pointed towards a rickety wooden gate at the far end of the courtyard. "That's the way out," she whispered.

Together, they crept towards the gate, their movements silent and swift. Just as Amelia reached for the latch, a bloodcurdling scream ripped through the night air, chilling them to the bone.

They exchanged a panicked look, the scream a grim confirmation of David's fate. Grief threatened to overwhelm Amelia, but she forced it down, shoving it deep into a compartment of her mind. There would be time for mourning later, if there was a later.

With trembling hands, Amelia fumbled with

Nine

Into the Storm

With trembling hands, Amelia fumbled with the rusty latch of the creaking wooden gate. The scream that had pierced the night echoed in her ears, a constant reminder of the price of their escape. Beside her, the young woman shivered, her gaze darting nervously towards the imposing walls of Blackwood Manor.

Finally, the latch yielded with a groan, and the gate swung open with a screech. Beyond lay a dense thicket of trees, their branches clawing at the stormy night sky. The wind howled through the leaves, a mournful cry that mirrored the turmoil in Amelia's heart.

"This way," the young woman whispered, urgency lacing her voice. She darted into the undergrowth, disappearing into the tangled mess of branches and foliage.

Amelia hesitated for a moment, her eyes scanning the periphery for any sign of pursuit. The silence was broken only by the howling wind and the distant rumble of thunder. With a deep breath, she plunged into the thicket, the sharp prick of thorns tearing at her clothes.

The darkness of the woods was absolute, the path barely discernible under the dense canopy of leaves. Amelia stumbled forward, guided by the faint rustling sounds made by the young woman ahead. They moved with an urgency born of fear, the damp earth sucking at their shoes with every step.

As they ventured deeper into the woods, the storm intensified. Rain lashed down in sheets, blurring the already indistinct path. Lightning ripped across the sky, momentarily illuminating the gnarled branches and twisted roots that seemed to reach out like skeletal fingers.

Amelia tripped over a hidden root, sprawling onto the muddy ground. Pain shot through her ankle, but she ignored it, scrambling back to her feet. She couldn't afford to slow down, not with whoever occupied Blackwood Manor possibly searching for them.

Suddenly, the young woman stopped, her hand outstretched towards a towering oak tree. A hollow throb echoed from within its ancient trunk, a sound that seemed oddly rhythmic.

"This is it," she whispered, her voice barely audible over the howling wind.

With a look of determination, the young woman began pushing against a loose section of bark, revealing a hidden cavity within the tree. The space was just large enough for a person to squeeze through.

"This is an old escape route," the young woman explained, her voice strained. "It leads to the abandoned mines on the outskirts of town."

Amelia stared at the dark opening, a surge of claustrophobia threatening to overwhelm her. But the thought of facing their pursuers was even more terrifying.

"What about you?" Amelia asked, her voice barely a whisper.

The young woman shook her head. "I can't go with you. They'll be looking for me too."

A flicker of gratitude sparked within Amelia. This young woman, whoever she was, had risked her life to help them escape. She reached into her pocket and pulled out a small locket, the only valuable she had left.

"Take this," Amelia said, pressing the locket into the young woman's hand. "It's not much, but..."

The young woman's eyes widened in surprise. "This is..." She cut herself off, her voice thick with emotion.

"Just a token of my thanks," Amelia finished, her voice hoarse. "Please, be careful."

With a final nod, the young woman disappeared into the hollowed-out trunk. Amelia took a deep breath, the weight of the locket a comforting presence in her empty palm. She had no idea what awaited her in the abandoned mines, but it seemed preferable to the dangers that lurked behind.

Steeling herself, Amelia squeezed through the narrow opening, the rough bark scraping against her skin. The darkness within was absolute, the only sound her own ragged breaths. She closed her eyes, the image of David's determined face flashing in her mind.

"I'll find you, David," she whispered into the darkness, her voice a vow laced with grief and defiance. Then, pushing forward into the unknown, she began to crawl.

Ten

Echoes in the Tunnels

The cramped tunnel stretched before Amelia like a black maw, the air thick with dust and the stench of damp earth. Each ragged breath scraped against her raw throat, the taste of metallic fear lingering on her tongue. The locket felt cool against her palm, a fragile reminder of the young woman who had aided their escape.

Clawing her way forward on hands and knees, Amelia navigated the uneven terrain. The rough stone floor dug into her exposed knees, but the pain was a dull ache compared to the crushing weight of despair threatening to engulf her.

David's final scream echoed in her memory, a haunting reminder of the cost of their rebellion. Grief threatened to cripple her, but she pushed it down, fueled by a desperate determination to survive.

The passage seemed endless, the darkness absolute. Time lost all meaning, measured only by the rhythmic rasp of her breaths and the occasional drip-drip of water from unseen crevices.

Just when despair clawed at the edges of her sanity, a faint glimmer of light flickered ahead. As Amelia crawled closer, the glimmer resolved into the flickering flame of a single oil lamp, its meager light casting long, grotesque shadows on the damp walls.

The tunnel opened into a cavern of surprising size. The air hung heavy with the stale smell of disuse, and the only sound was the distant drip of water echoing off the cavern walls. A network of tunnels branched out in various directions, each passage an invitation to further darkness.

Uncertainty gnawed at Amelia. Which way to go? Without a map or any sense of direction, she felt adrift in an underground labyrinth.

Suddenly, a low rumbling sound echoed through the cavern, sending shivers down Amelia's spine. Her heart hammered against her ribs, her mind conjuring images of unseen creatures lurking in the shadows.

Cupping a hand around the flickering flame of the oil lamp, Amelia crept forward, her senses on high alert. The cavern floor was littered with rusted tools and remnants of mining equipment, stark reminders of a bygone era.

As she continued, the flickering light revealed faded markings on the cavern walls – cryptic symbols and arrows etched into the rough stone. Was this a clue, a message left behind by previous occupants?

A flicker of hope sparked within Amelia. Maybe this wasn't a dead end after all. Maybe these markings held the key to navigating the labyrinthine tunnels.

Squinting at the symbols, she tried to decipher their meaning. Some resembled animals, others geometric shapes. Were they a directional code, a map etched into the very walls?

With renewed purpose, Amelia began tracing the symbols, murmuring them silently under her breath – stag, arrow, serpent. Slowly, a tentative plan began to form in her mind.

Following the sequence of the symbols, she chose a tunnel that branched off to the west. The passage narrowed again, the air growing colder and thicker with dust. But Amelia pressed forward, the flicker of the oil lamp her only solace in the oppressive darkness.

After what felt like an eternity, the passage opened into another cavern. This one seemed larger, the faint echoes of movement reaching her ears. A sliver of unease slithered up her spine. Was she alone in these tunnels, or were there other inhabitants?

Crouching low to the ground, Amelia crept forward, her movements silent and cautious. As she rounded a corner, the flickering light of her lamp revealed a scene that froze her blood in her veins.

A group of men, their faces obscured by the shadows, huddled around a table lit by a flickering lantern. Papers and maps were spread across the surface, and their hushed conversation carried the unmistakable air of conspiracy. These were no ordinary miners. These were powerful figures, the very ones she and David sought to expose.

Understanding dawned on Amelia. The abandoned mines were not just a refuge, but a hidden headquarters for the corrupt elite. A wave of nausea washed over her. She had stumbled upon the heart of the darkness, a place where secrets were kept and power was wielded in the shadows.

But before she could react, a voice cut through the tense silence, shattering the fragile veil of her invisibility.

"Who's there?" a gruff voice boomed, followed by the clatter of a drawn weapon. The men around the table whirled around, their faces etched with surprise and a flicker of something more sinister.

Amelia stood frozen, trapped in the unforgiving glare of the lantern light. Her heart hammered against her ribs, a frantic drumbeat echoing in the cavernous silence. She had walked into a lion's den, and there would be no easy escape.

Eleven

A Web of Lies

Amelia stood paralyzed, the flickering lantern light painting grotesque shadows across her face. The men around the table, their expressions morphing from surprise to suspicion, tightened their grips on various weapons – a crowbar, a hunting knife, a glint of polished metal that could only be a gun.

One man, taller and broader than the others, stepped forward, his face shrouded in darkness. "Who are you? How did you get in here?" His voice was a low growl, laced with menace.

Amelia's mind raced, searching for a coherent lie, an explanation that wouldn't reveal her true purpose. Fear choked her voice, but she forced herself to speak.

"I... I got lost," she stammered, her voice barely a whisper. "I was wandering in the woods and stumbled upon an opening. I didn't mean to intrude."

The men exchanged skeptical glances. A younger man, his face etched with nervous energy, scoffed. "Lost? Down here? Don't make me laugh."

Amelia ignored his outburst, her eyes darting towards the scattered papers on the table. Her heart lurched. A glimpse of familiar symbols, similar to the ones etched on the cavern walls, peeked out from under a worn leather-bound book. These symbols, her only clue through the labyrinthine tunnels, were now in the hands of her worst enemies.

"Show me your hands," the leader commanded, his voice leaving no room for argument.

Amelia slowly raised her hands, wincing as the harsh light glinted off the locket clutched tightly in her palm. The leader's eyes narrowed as they fell on the locket.

"Where did you get that?" he demanded, his voice tight.

Panic flared in Amelia's chest. Could this be a connection? Did this locket hold a key to their secrets? She feigned innocence.

"It's just a family heirloom," she choked out, desperately trying to keep her voice steady.

The leader's gaze remained fixed on the locket, his brow furrowed in concentration. The tension in the room was thick enough to choke on.

Just as Amelia thought her flimsy story might hold, the younger man sneered. "She's lying, boss. Look at her. She's shaking like a leaf."

The leader turned his attention back to Amelia, his eyes gleaming with a dangerous glint. "Perhaps," he conceded, his voice devoid of warmth. "But there's something about that locket that troubles me."

He reached out, his hand hovering a mere inch from Amelia's. Fear threatened to paralyze her, but a flicker of defiance sparked within her. She wouldn't let them intimidate her.

"Don't touch me," she spat, her voice surprisingly strong. "I told you, it's nothing. Just let me go."

The leader's lips curled into a cruel smile. "I don't think so. Not until we figure out what you're doing here and how much you've seen."

A hand clamped down on Amelia's shoulder, sending a jolt of pain through her. Another man, his face hidden beneath a wide-brimmed hat, roughly shoved her towards a rickety chair in the corner.

Desperate for a diversion, Amelia glanced around the cavern, searching for an escape route. Her gaze fell on a tunnel branching out just beyond the circle of light cast by the lantern. It was a long shot, but it was her only hope.

Just as the leader began to speak, Amelia lunged forward, knocking over a chair in the process. The men were caught off guard by her sudden movement, momentarily distracted by the clatter and her desperate struggle against the man who held her captive.

Seizing the opportunity, Amelia twisted free and bolted towards the darkened tunnel. The men roared after her, their angry shouts echoing through the cavern.

Adrenaline coursed through Amelia's veins, fueling her frantic dash. She didn't know where the tunnel led, but anywhere was better than facing the wrath of those men.

The passage narrowed quickly, the air growing stale and thick with dust. The sound of her pursuers' footsteps faded with each step she took deeper into the darkness. But just as she began to believe she might outrun them, a deafening crack echoed through the tunnel, followed by a shower of falling debris.

The tunnel had collapsed behind her, cutting off her escape route and plunging her into an even deeper darkness, a suffocating silence broken only by the ragged gasps of her own breath.

Lost, trapped, and surrounded by enemies, a wave of despair washed over Amelia. She had stumbled upon the truth, but at what cost?

Twelve

Echoes of Hope

Days bled into weeks, the oppressive darkness of the collapsed tunnel becoming Amelia's only reality. Hunger gnawed at her stomach, thirst parched her throat, and despair threatened to consume her. The flickering memory of David, his determined face and final sacrifice, was the only thing that kept her clinging to a sliver of hope.

One day, a faint sound reached her ears, a rhythmic tapping that echoed through the tunnel. At first, she dismissed it as a trick of her mind, a cruel illusion born of isolation. But the tapping persisted, a steady beat that seemed to beckon her closer.

With renewed determination, Amelia crawled towards the sound, her body aching, her spirit a fragile ember. The tapping grew louder, and eventually, she reached a point where the wall seemed different, the stone less solid.

With trembling hands, she scraped away at the loose rocks, revealing a small opening. Squinting through the gap, she saw… light. A shaft of golden sunlight streamed down, illuminating a narrow passage beyond.

Tears welled up in Amelia's eyes, a mixture of relief and exhaustion. Using the last vestiges of her strength, she clawed her way through the opening, tumbling onto the damp earth floor of a hidden clearing bathed in sunlight.

The clearing was a small oasis within the depths of the earth. A canopy of ferns and moss covered the ceiling, filtering the sunlight into a dappled pattern on the forest floor. A stream gurgled merrily through the clearing, offering the promise of life-giving water.

Amelia drank deeply, the cool water washing away the dust and despair that had clung to her for so long. As she lay there, gathering her strength, a rustle in the bushes sent a jolt through her.

A figure emerged from the undergrowth, a young woman with eyes filled with concern. It was the girl from Blackwood Manor, the one who had guided Amelia to the hidden escape route.

"You're alive!" she exclaimed, her voice filled with relief. "I never thought…"

Amelia managed a weak smile. "Neither did I. But you… how did you find me?"

The young woman explained that after Amelia disappeared, she had managed to escape Blackwood Manor. Determined to find David, she had followed the markings on the walls, eventually stumbling upon the collapsed tunnel. She had spent days searching the area, a glimmer of hope fueling her determination.

Together, they explored the clearing, finding a small cave hidden behind a curtain of vines. Inside, a meager collection of supplies offered basic necessities – blankets, dried food, and a lantern. This must have been David's hidden retreat, his secret haven within the labyrinthine tunnels.

As they settled in for the night, huddled together for warmth, Amelia learned the young woman's name was Lily. She had witnessed the corruption firsthand, her family ostracized and threatened for speaking out.

A fragile bond formed between them, a shared sense of loss intertwined with a flicker of defiant hope. David might be gone, but his sacrifice had not been in vain. They knew the truth, and they wouldn't let it be buried in the darkness.

The days that followed were a blur of planning and preparation. Lily, with her knowledge of the tunnels and the town's underbelly, became Amelia's guide and confidante. They pieced together the information Amelia had gleaned from the men in the cavern, using it to solidify their plan.

One moonlit night, after weeks of careful preparation, Amelia and Lily emerged from the hidden entrance to the tunnels. They were no longer the scared, lost individuals who had stumbled into the darkness. They were fueled by a shared purpose, an unwavering determination to expose the web of lies that had choked Driftwood Bay for so long.

Their journey had just begun, fraught with danger and uncertainty. But as they walked towards the town under the cloak of night, a flicker of light burned in their eyes – the echo of a truth waiting to be unearthed.

Milton Keynes UK
Ingram Content Group UK Ltd.
UKHW040650060824
446478UK00028B/80

9 782912 968586